Book of Words, Definitions, and Phrases

Vernon L. Mann, Esq.

GRATITUDE & ACKNOWLEDGEMENTS

I want to thank the Creator for making all of this possible. Next, I'd like to acknowledge the unwavering guidance of my two loving parents who, despite the world's perception of me, remained heroes to their baby boy. Their efforts to steer me in the right direction has been the driving force behind all my achievements and success.

My parents, Jimmy Mann and Mary Alice McNeil-Mann, are my heart and every day I work to emulate their courage while avoiding their errors.

What it really boils down to asking yourself who is going to take the time to tell you what you need to know? One person that took the time to tell me what I needed to know was Monk a.k.a Ronnie Funches. He was the best friend of my oldest brother James. I'm sad to say Monk recently passed away. Like the rest of my family, Monk never stopped working to inspire and help make me a better person.

I would like to acknowledge my older sisters Sheba, Tempie, Janice, and Candace and then my big brother Derek coupled with my two little sisters Kimmie and Angel. While I'm at it, I would also like to take this time to thank so many other family members like Boobie, Brendale, Cookie, Vaughn, Claudia, Caroline, along with my numerous other cousins. I would also like to acknowledge my many nieces and nephews like Lakey, Juicey, Jewel, Iesha, Allison, Ashley, Tavis, both of my nieces name Sabrina, Precious, Vincent, Eric, Stevie, Aquarius, Jamel, Caprice, DeShawn, Travis, Rajean, Jada, Kareem, Courtney, Rashawn, Dwayne, Dwight, Davon, Imere, D'Andre, Da'Quise, De'ontae, Elquan, Kaiden, Kaleif, Clarissa, & Khalique. I'd also like to thank close family friends for their inspiration throughout the years.

That would include, but would not be limited to, Ms. Newton and Ms. Watts-Bey for their continued love and unwavering support that they've shown me for over 30 years. I'd also like to "Big-Up" Shawn and Todd Watts-Bey. I'd also like to thank both Imani's - my daughter and my God-daughter, along with my God-son Aiden.

I'd like to thank some of my most dearest friends, like Peter Bradley (the man who taught me the strategy to do what I love to do everyday, even if it's just a little bit every day).

I'd also like to show gratitude and acknowledgement to some of my real good friends such as Haneef Abdullah, CPA, William "Bill" Hunt, Professor at St. Lawrence University, Grandmaster Caz of The Cold Crush Brothers, Levy Moore, David Boatswain, my good buddy, Mr. Wayne Scully, and Miles Davis' son, Gregory Davis who was gracious enough to include me in his book as well.

Speaking of books, I'd like to send a very special thanks out to the Substantive Editor of this book, A~LaKisha Eure' of EUREthics Editing House, for her intellectual and creative input. Also for working so diligently in making this book into the vehicle to launch my new career as a Next Level Mettle Motivational Speaker. Thank you to all of the above for being ever so patient and showing me so much love.

Words of Introduction

How do you know if you're right or if you're really wrong? Why would you think you're right, *when* you've been wrong all along? When right can be wrong and wrong can feel right, HOW WOULD YOU KNOW?

The solution comes by leaving space, just in case you make a few very human mistakes. THAT is how you know. THAT is how we all grow.

Greetings.

I am pleased that you are here to hear what I'm so excited to share.

I am Mr. Vernon Mann. I'm unique. I was a wayward youth that morphed into a repeat offender – that evolved into an attorney.

I was born, bred, and misled in Brownsville Brooklyn. It is a hood that is not so civil and where an abundance of drama occurred. It was an unneighborly hood where recidivism was a common phenomena. In fact, studies were conducted on folks like me – a former convict from one of the impoverished inner city Apartheid-like areas of NYC. I was one of the disproportionate minorities that unceremoniously became state property by joining the overwhelmingly melanated prison population.

It is unfathomable that out of the approximately 250 neighborhoods in The Big Apple, that a mere seven neighborhoods in NYC provide a whopping 85% of the NYS Upstate Prison population. It sounds incredulous but it is the unbelievable truth.

That life was my claim to shame. Praise God, that I'm not the same.

The 80s and 90s were periods likened to war times. I have been through the hell of urban warfare. I have been through the fire and I am so grateful that I don't smell like smoke.

This book is for people who want to be better, and not be bitter. It is for those who recognize that they have other people to consider before deciding whether or not to risk it alllll, by pulling that symbolic trigger.

This book is filled with mechanisms and road maps that may be able to aid you too from falling into some of life's trip ups and traps. This is a book of jewels and gems that can serve as life-long tools.

You will find wisdom from the sages in between the pages of my personal book of Words, Definitions, and Phrases. I pray that as it helps you, you'll graciously pass it on to aid others in navigating the inevitable pitfalls in life.

How do I know that this book can radically transform your life and help you to become a better person? Well for ten years I was a recidivist - a proud one. I went in and out of jail at a regrettable frequency. Regrettably but justifiably, I received very few visitors during my detainments. Thus allowing me a lot of time to think about my predicament. One of the many things that I've learned in that process is that your definition of "strange" will likely change as you go through the dilemmas of life. When I finally decided that I needed to implement a plan and commit to making changes in the way I lived my life – my thoughts became increasingly clearer and more positive.

I started my evolution by switching up my language and realizing how words affect behavior.

Hence the title: Book of *Words, Definitions, and Phrases.*

This book is purposely short in length but packed with ideas. Many of us actually prefer to refrain from reading, if we can avoid it. In fact, according to statistics, "The percentage of the U.S. adult population reading any books has declined by 7 percent over the past decade and has dropped dramatically over the past 20 years. Less than half of the adult American population now reads literature." It seems safe to conclude that there is a correlation between reading and affluence. "86% of people with an annual household income of $75,000 a year read at least one book every year." Therefore, I wrote a book that is concise and pleasurable to read. Considering the findings on the reduction of the average

American Attention Span – It is quite skimmable too. As an author I was compelled to write the type of book that readers wish were widely available. My book is not too wordy. Though the words are few, the impact can be great.

It can affect many facets of your life, yet it is easy to comprehend. It is brief, handy, and "to the point." I love how it has positively impacted my life. I strongly believe that your Book will bring you the same joy and desire to share.

That is exactly what this handbook offers to you and all the subsequent readers who will benefit because of your generosity to share knowledge by turning the phrase, "Each One Teach One" into action. You are contributing to a cycle of growth simply by perusing and using this book, writing your own book, and then sharing the process. I hope this concept becomes widely accepted, which will also result in increased readership. A literate society benefits all of its members.

This book is a demonstration of how you too can, and should, start defining your own words and phrases while giving them specific values. I encourage you to ponder the words and phrases that have brought you success and compile them into a concrete legacy for future generations. Affording our offspring a head start by not having to start from scratch gives greater significance to the phrase "Let Us See Your Legacy." By writing your very own book, your descendants will be able to read the words that you intended to be used for their betterment. Intentionally passing on such information long before our offspring are even born or even thought of – is an expression of authentic love.

You're about to read a book that's short yet powerful. It is possibly one of the best investments you could have possibly procured. These words, definitions, and phrases are derived from my most humbling experiences. Getting better requires a method that has been tried and tested. Many of the words that I have collected helped me to look at life from different perspectives.

For example, many people do not acknowledge that at birth they were equipped with a compendium of instructions. The three books I'm referring to, once compiled together, can help you grapple with what happened before you got here, with how you got here, and why so many others are not here. There is but one caveat to the compendium of instructions booklets ~ while I may not be able to prove they are 100% right, I am equally sure that you can't prove they are 100% wrong.

What am I referring to? Well, I am very cognisant that everyone has free will to decide whether or not they believe in a higher power. However, you cannot deny that people lived before you existed. Within the aforementioned instructions are a multitude of stories that relate to several topics and situations.

Some of the stories convey how the original people went astray. Others shed light on age-old conflicts. If you haven't guessed it by now, the names of these compendiums of instructional strategies are

The Old Testament, The New Testament. and The Last Testament. Your very own Book of Words, Definitions, and Phrases will act as your Personal Testament. We all have testimonies about obstacles and situations that we have experienced or may still be grappling with.

Your personal Book of Words, Definitions, and Phrases will not only act as the culmination of the Three Testaments, but it may help others to better assess and address their own situations. This handbook can serve as an easy template for you to follow while you fortify your legacy.

Before I move on to the crux of this discourse, I will make this disclaimer: Everything is not for everybody. Period. So if you insist on being a bitter person, then this book is definitely not for you. I'm very sorry for your loss. All others, let's get started.

Who was I?

I used to be a person who always swore that I was certain. I wholeheartedly believed this fallacy. That was until I got stuck in the revolving door of the penal system. I was going back and forth to jail until I realized that what I was doing was not working for my good. That epiphany occurred when I was incarcerated during my last bid. That is when I was given a dossier on the man who would forever change my life - Mr. Reginald F. Lewis. If you've never heard of him, then you should immediately stop reading this book and pick up his life-changing book,- *Why Should White Men Have All The Fun?* Mr. Lewis was serious about his business. I love this guy. This man changed my life overnight!

Here was a man who looked like me, from his complexion down to the gap between his two front teeth. I voraciously read about him while I was incarcerated. His book made me believe that if I changed my life around *just one more time that* I would not fail. Mr. Lewis helped me to materialize my vision into what I ultimately would become - an attorney.

To appreciate the conflicts I was facing, you would first have to understand the gravity of life as an inner city youth. In Brownsville, Brooklyn it is rare for a young Black boy to grow up to become a mature man. Many boys did not plan for adulthood - including me. I was convinced that I was going to die young. I felt endangered because of my race and because of the neighborhood from which I came. A study was conducted that supported the belief that Black and Latino people from the seven depressed neighborhoods in NYC could not be trusted. During my crass past life I too was one of them, so I concur.

It may sound strange but desperate people do desperate things.

I was convicted of three felonies. Based on what my fellow wayward brethren were cautioning me about and coupled with what I already knew, it became crystal clear that the system was failing me. Or was I failing the system? I thought jail was the culmination of criminality and that it would be the beginning of rehabilitation from wayward ways. When in fact, it is often quite the opposite. However, I've learned there is no such thing as rehabilitation without using your limitless imagination.

With that being said, let me tell you why I am here.

My aim is clear. I want this book to illuminate how a Black man, born in Brownsville, Brooklyn who possessed multiple felonies became a corporate, entertainment, and tax attorney. How did that happen to a guy who just years prior, was rapping at the World Famous Apollo Theater? I'll tell you how. I remained focused and continued to adhere to Reginald F. Lewis's essential message – Giving Up is Not Allowed.

I guess my job is obvious. My job is to encourage you to, "Buy into You." I got better and if you're willing to do the work, then you can get better too. Forget about how you may look. Appearance is a superficial focus. Becoming a better you has more to do with your mentality and less about your physicality.

Look, If you want to move, it requires that you are willing to do the hard work in order to improve. I believe it was Les Brown who once said, "The hardest job you'll ever do is the job of working on you." So ladies and gents, I'll tell you what I'm going to do. I am simply going to tell you my truths.

I am not proud of some of my experiences but nor am I ashamed. They helped me to evolve into a principled man, and I am no longer the same.

Despite it being the basis of relaying information, I am fully aware that most people prefer to not read. Therefore, I purposely made this book compact and portable to address this conundrum. Much like Benjamin Franklin's pocket-sized hardcover edition of his thirteen Moral Virtues posthumously published in 1791, this book was meant to be handy. It is full of quotes and genuinely meant to help all folks whether or not you're a counselor, consultant, or a coach.

Here is my approach:

Welcome to Practical Wisdom at a Glance

THE DEFINITIONS

Without fail, life events have shown me what I now know to be true - that "definitions" only makes sense (cents) if it holds worth (value). Words are the Building Blocks of communication. Words can construct simple sentences or complex dissertations. Words are multifaceted and mean multiple things. Words are powerful. We use words for a plethora of purposes as we experience the fullness of life. As we learn and grow, our definitions and usage may change. With that being understood, these words are mine at this moment in time.

How will these definitions help you? They may help you to make adjustments. amends, and assessments.

Hopefully they can allow you to right what went left and make some wrongs right.

More importantly, understanding words and their meaning can help you make better choices. We all want to develop better ways to choose and use words. Especially when selecting partners, lovers, and friends. Definitions can point us in the right direction, enabling us to set positive and progressive objectives. So dear reader, please let me know if you find this book beneficial, or if you have constructive criticism that you'd like for me to consider. Either way,

I'd be more than happy to hear your feedback because, though people may not be receptive to it - we all need that.

A = ACT AS "IF"... UNTIL YOU BECOME!

____

____

____

____

____

____

____

B = B.I.B.L.E. - LET IT GUIDE YOU - BASIC. INSTRUCTIONS. Before. Leaving. Earth.

____

____

____

____

____

C = CHOICES ARE VOICES. THEY "SPEAK" WHEN YOU exercise them.

D = D.U.M.B. = DON'T. UNDERESTIMATE. MY. Brilliance. D can also stand for Discipline.

Discipline is more than just positioning. Discipline starts with genuine listening.

E = Excuses only satisfy those who make them and promises are meaningless if you frivolously break them.

F = Frequency - Is what you get to keep of me when you tune into my vibe. My frequency leaves memories.

____

____

____

____

G = GETTING BETTER OR GROWING BIGGER.

Either one works best when like minded people do it together.

____

____

____

____

____

____

____

H = HUMILITY - NO MATTER WHAT ANYONE THINKS, humility is strength, shown by having the ability to practice restraint. Do you have the amazing ability to practice humility?

____

____

____

I= Interest is a place to enter and rest.

J = Like Jesus, our leaders shouldn't judge a person exclusively by their outwardly features. One's character is a much better calculus of characteristics.

____

____

____

____

____

____

K = KEEP YOUR WORD CLUB IS ONE OF THE BEST CLUBS that you could be a part of. It is your bond.

____

____

____

____

____

____

____

L = LOVE IS WHEN YOU WANT A PERSON TO BE ALIVE ON Earth. In contrast to Like. Love is not just wanting a person to be on Earth, it's also wanting to be around them because you love them and value their worth.

____

____

____

____

____

____

____

____

M = MEMORY - THE WAY IN WHICH WE SACREDLY RECALL events in order to recapture the whole experience.

____

____

____

____

____

____

____

N = NONE OF US ARE SMARTER THAN ALL OF US! WE come together as a team to play the game because collectively we are stronger and smarter than when we operate as individuals.

____

O = Options - If you have some, there's a high probability that your future will blossom!

P = P.E.A.C.E.- Please Educate Allah's Children Every day!

____

____

____

____

____

____

____

Q = Quran - It's a widely held belief that the Quran is the sacred text that the Creator provided to respond to other books that are either confused or untrue.

____

____

____

____

____

____

____

R = Respect - really means to look and consider to whom you are talking to and regarding them accordingly.

S = S.I.Y.C.K. - You are S.I.Y.C.K. when there's "Something Inside You Can't Kick."

T = Torah - Believers say it is the first scripture

that created the over- all picture of the Creator's law, unlike anything man has seen before.

____

____

____

____

____

____

____

U = UNKNOWN IS THE LACK OF A REPEATED PHENOMENA which usually results in fear. The unknown reminds us not to mistake the ability to predict with the ability to control what we don't know.

____

____

____

____

____

____

V = Vibes should determine whether you stay or leave – from whomever, wherever, and whenever.

____

____

____

____

____

____

____

____

W = When dealing with shiesty people, having a "Who Could Care Less" attitude makes you victorious. Don't be stressed by their "mess."

____

____

____

____

____

____

____

Y = You. There are three of you; the you that the world knows, the you that your family and friends know and lastly, the you that only you know. I'm speaking to the latter.

____

____

____

____

____

____

____

____

The Phrases

Much like Ben Franklin, I didn't create all of these expressions. However, I decided to modify them by putting my unique twist on them, to make them more applicable and memorable.

Over a period of time, my hope is that this work will inspire other sisters and brothers to respond in kind with their own words, definitions and phrases that they've gravitated toward over time. Many of us don't know that the etymological root of the word mathematics means "that which is learnt." Therefore, no matter your entry level into the concept of learning, I really hope that you can learn at least one useful thing that you didn't know before you read this book. Being able to learn and use essential tools makes us all better, wiser, and a little less confused. We have to consider whose views we'll eventually choose to use, to make the world a better place. It's always a good look to learn something new from a valuable book. Hopefully, you'll consider this as one of them.

- By now you should know me, V. Mann, the self-proclaimed one-trick pony, who's here to do one thing and one thing only. I'm here to "sell you on you" by finding out what it is that you love to do!

- One of the many things the story of Reginald F Lewis instilled in me was the idea built around the possibility that I can do a better job at being me.

- When it comes to dropping seeds, does your experience align with your challenges and your needs? What about your deeds? If not, act as if- until you become.

- Ideas: If you can package it and fashion it in a way that no one else imagined it–your odds of becoming rich are absolutely fabulous.

- It is an intimate private decision when one gets pregnant with an idea or a vision. Only you can decide if you will bring it into fruition by starting a viable business.

- When you start looking around for what's missing, it's probably the product, service, or idea that you never brought into fruition.

- Basically, if you are looking for a solution, it involves creating an idea and being flawless in your execution.

- There is power in ideas. In fact, post incarceration my business plan has held up for well over 30 years. Ideas + Action + Integrity = LONGEVITY.

- By now it should be crystal clear what we're doing here. We are choosing to rank our ideas over our fears.

- A secret is only a secret if you are able to keep it. Don't play yourself cheap by asking someone else to keep a secret that you yourself couldn't keep.

- Life will definitely test the boundaries of your character. If it hasn't, don't worry you'll get your turn. Instead of being overly concerned, just remember what Nelson Mandela said, "I never lose, I either win or I learn."

- What you want to do is - not make excuses. Persevere because when you're good at what you do, you might produce something timeless and exclusive– that ends up reflecting you.

- Everything has a place. Keep items in its place and then you'll never misplace it or have to replace it.

- Come prepared –not scared.

- No matter how cute, slick, or witty you may be - always remember, God doesn't like ugly and HE AIN'T CRAZY ABOUT PRETTY!

- We should all pay homage to our civic responsibility to expand and share knowledge.

- If you want help - start by defining who you are to yourself.

- "Good Tunes" are a great tool to elevate your mood and to lighten up any room.

- The hard work is not finished until you have a carefully Crafted Public Image (C.P.I.) Your C.P.I. is the KEY to how the rest of the world will eventually "see" you.

- Keep your network tight. If you don't want the demons to seep through, try to surround yourself with people who know how to treat you.

- Sometimes you may have to take a loss and say F*** it, in order to escape arguing with crabs stuck in the proverbial bucket.

- Any human being trying to achieve a dream, no matter how high the mountain, must be willing to climb it. This is what I call a, "Black Wall Street" mindset.

- When you're approachable, you make others want to be close to you– hoping one day to be as dope as you.

- Good company has the potential to make memories more memorable.

- If you want people to vividly hear what they just heard, sometimes you just have to add a few images to your words.

- With certain things it's not even worth debating it., especially if it's widely known that it's not even a true statement.

- If you don't want to end up being a mere photo copy, remember the good book and do not answer a fool to his own folly.

- After having been a wayward youth, I've learned and I've grown. It's almost like coming back from a hideaway and not expecting to be welcomed home.

- When it comes to Happiness and Success, at best many of us just aren't sure anymore. Why? It's because we don't know what it looks like, which means we don't know what to look for.

- The goal is to win, without having to throw caution to the wind – that's if you don't want anyone to get hurt in the end.

- Be confident that you've done your personal best, so after you've made a critical decision you're still able to pass the "Mirror Test".

- If the Creator sent you someone that makes you better, why are you still so bitter? Is it not a blessing? Just a little something to consider. If and when they leave, can you really and truly call them the quitter? Hmm, go figure.

- There are Black faces in high places, that is well and fine. My question is, why is the Black quality of life continuing to decline?

- When it comes to who we vote for, I think along the lines of Malcolm X and Bob Law. "Do you want a superior candidate or do you want money and a date?" Tricks and lies are nothing new so just choose the superior candidate that is best suited to represent you.

- Candidates are characters, so your support should not be official until you first confirm that their goals align with the issues.

- Conversations go nowhere without a clear understanding of why all parties are there.

- As a guy, I can get pregnant too. This is why I actually cheer when I give birth to a business idea. A human baby can develop over 9 months before it appears. However, one other thing you should consider is that an EIN is also a 9 digit number. Coincidence or is it now making sense?

- What happens to your goals and dreams once life starts pulling at the seams? I'll tell you what to do. Just remember, many things sound reasonable until you do the math and think them through.

- Do you change your dreams and put your goals on hold? However, consider that if you opt to hold it, one day you may not be able to control it?

- Credibility comes with work worthy of credit. It's a good thing, if you can get it.

- The notable Ben Frank said, "Cheap or free labor makes some folks feeble and in disfavor." The way I figure it, that's also relevant today. Why not consider it?

- To fortify your financial foundation, Blockchain should be the next train leaving the station. This is the lead car that can lay tracks down for the future applications that are sure to come. Crypto is just a test run. Watch and see what happens to the next one.

- Take note that practice is not always positive. Be aware of people who practice creating false equivalencies in order to get you distracted and moving backwards.

- False equivalencies cannot exist on the Blockchain because it independently verifies the integrity in question. It feels as though Blockchain will become the digital equivalent to factory seals.

- You may pay more in taxes because you allow what you think and believe to be stronger than the actual facts. If that describes you, then you need to check that.

- The IRS objective is quite simple to follow and as equally hard to confuse: "Depending on the style used, the beating continues until morale improves."

- Imagine a client telling me that he didn't know if he was being prosecuted for being a journalist or for being Black. Well your imagination is not needed – it actually happened. That was a conundrum that I couldn't explain.

- I don't want you to think people emerge purely out of obscurity. Oh no, they must first confirm and fortify their position.

- Technological trends indicate we will see many things change as more of us gravitate toward Blockchain. Even politics won't be the same. In fact, the African American community's colloquialism for such a thing is, Game Recognise Game.

- Without question, one of your most valuable possessions is your time. Try not to waste yours. I can promise you that I won't waste mine.

- Money may or may not bring you happiness. Be careful where you overlook because big things sometimes come in small packages.

- Others say money isn't everything, I don't have to tell you that it helps. If you don't agree, that's fine. Just get out of my way and let me see for myself.

- Reasonable people, address their vexation by managing their expectations.

- A lady friend once said, "Staying humble and hungry will help you avoid being broke and lonely."

- How do you distinguish between wrong from right, when for every meal you have to fuss and fight?

- In life, most of us are just looking for a sustainable model, something that's simple and easy to follow. It may be smooth or it may be the proverbial "hard pill to swallow."

- The definitions, words, and phrases that we choose to use are most effective when they communicate our views and respective perspectives.

- Blockchain is about clarity, trust, and transparency.

- Your brain is your biggest asset and investment, and your brain is nothing to mess with. Keeping a sound mind is most excellent.

- Some people have good advice to give and sincerely I'm all for it. Be careful about taking financial advice from those who are not qualified and obviously unfit to offer it.

- Consistency and the ability to look at your life differently, as if it was meant to be, will allow you to build relationships that are built to last. It is in contrast to the same old ones built around errors and remnants of your past.

- Venture Capitalism has always been interesting to me. Before your money is gone, make sure you know what you're spending it on. You should Know, speak, and comprehend the language of Term Sheets.

- Leadership in action requires that you listen to your intuition – trusting that following your conscience is indeed the right decision.

- I may not control which way or which day I "go", however, I can attempt to control how I'll be remembered though.

- My hope is that you're able to cope. Stay focused ,though at times life may seem quite hopeless.

- I'm not spending time trying to hate ya or debate ya. Instead, I'm focused on Father Time and Mother Nature.

- Even when your heart is in the right place, how do you know when your head is? By defining YOUR definition of leverage.

- Music is an effective channeling source to help us collect and express our internal thoughts.

- Some rappers are so good at rhyming without even trying, it's almost like they're mining for diamonds while spitting out jewels for the rest of the world to use.

- It's never too late to start working on your own book of Words, Definitions, and Phrases. Be so bold, daring, and courageous that people can't wait to dig through the pages.

- When you step into certain places that don't appear to be the safest, one of the first things you should do is manage your expectations.

- We deprive ourselves when we fail to do what the Earth does every day – evolve.

- Peace and Drama. The key to distinguishing between the two lies in knowing which one is static and which one is a signal.

- I've had it. Had it with what? Not knowing the difference between math and mathematics.

- I'm hoping that the 45% of new businesses who fail during the first five years of being opened will one day realize that one thing that can keep them alive is the wisdom of an incubation system.

- When you get a little hype because you "made it", realize money isn't everything because you can still feel isolated.

- Someone can appear to be perfect on paper. Don't let them fake ya. Humans aren't perfect because perfection only exists in nature.

- Although I'm not seeking approval, it is my sincere hope that this book will move you to a better place to help you avoid making the same mistakes.

- Before you can master how to connect the dots, you must learn how to think outside of the box.

- To connect the dots you may have to look for the spots located on the outside of the box. That's how you focus and know what to watch.

- I'm not sure if you're hearing me! Your very own Book of Words, Definitions, & Phrases possess tools for you to use to bring forth prosperity as a form of currency.

- Life is full of mazes. It's almost like a good relationship that seems to always leave traces. These traces are defined by the lines on our smiling faces.

- What's cool, free, and never increases? Don't say it's love, because we pay for "love" every time our heart breaks into pieces.

- For people who are viewing the world through a prism of materialism, you have to be very careful with offering them any kind of constructive criticism.

- Options create more possibilities to make intelligent choices. Value your choices because they actually have voices. They are heard when you exercise them.

- If you ask a question and the answer doesn't touch your spirit, perhaps it is because the question was incoherent. Ask the right question to get the right answer.

- Trepidation has made Bitcoin an object of speculation. On the other hand and without exaggeration, Blockchain requires us to use and grow. The greatest nation on Earth is our endless imagination because it comes first.

- Anytime you say that you can't imagine something to be true you are professing the limitations of your imagination. You're risking self-fulfillment - making what you thought you couldn't do actually true.

- An investment is something you don't want to mess with, while it is in the process of being tried and tested.

• You know what's really rotten? That despite how you may
  have changed, bad practices and bad advice are seldom
  forgotten.

• Of course most of us were taught we should have enough
  courage to own up to our faults. But do we listen or is it
  too much of an imposition? Much like the lives we lead –
  it is usually an individual decision.

- Regardless of how we actually feel, sometimes we have to act like a book in order to eventually compose ourselves.

- Many foxes grow old and gray. However, have you ever heard an old fox say, "I'm not going to eat the hens in the hen house, at least not today?" A fox is going to be a fox. Ms. Maya Angelo verbalized it as, "When people tell you who they are, you should believe them."

- Racism only hurts when it works. In order for racism to not
hurt we have to make it ineffective. How do we do that?
Oh, I thought you'd never ask. It's called A.R.T. - A Racism
Tax. In the worst scenario, some bigots will have to lose
their property if they don't cease and desist racial practices.

- Doing the work is all about doing what you need to do
until you find out what you love to do. It should be

something you love so much that you're willing to do it for free. If there's a market for it and someone else is willing to pay you to do it – then pursue it. Once you find that, you've found happiness. Relish and cherish it.

- I once heard Rev. DeForest "Buster" Soaries say something profound–"Trouble is guaranteed because there are three types of people in the world, those who are about to get in trouble; those who are already in trouble; and those who just got out of trouble."

- My story is attached to what's evolving and relevant, reminiscent of how Black people went from picking cotton to picking a Black president.

- Much like energy that flows in different places, certain information is on a need to know basis.

- Math equals learning. How you apply it is what makes it mathematical.

- In order to truly bring about change, you have to learn to read more than just the obvious words. You have to learn to read people, places, and things, plus the "words" in between the lines.

- Taking the time to explore words shows the world how serious you are and how you'd like to be represented. It's much like being able to write your own Book of Words, Definitions & Phrases and letting the world know exactly what you intended.

- Merely entertaining certain matters should require some form of compensation – your time is not free.

- Your entry level into the conversation will determine its natural progression and ultimate destination. Come prepared, not scared because how and when you engage affects the outcome of affairs.

- No one is perfect, so there is always room for improvement. Are you respectful to the people who correct you? If you can't answer that, then it is safe to assume the answer is, "no." Keep in mind that it just may stunt your maturity and growth.

- There will always be factions that will cause distractions. Try to channel that energy toward what fuels your authentic passions.

- People have free-will to make choices, this is true. The irony is that we wouldn't have an economy if those same people weren't so darn predictable.

- If you're really trying to get better, I suggest that you try this: Spend at least a year doing your best to overcome personal biases.

- It's hard to finish a sentence without thinking about one's own security and financial Independence.

- Some of us have no choice other than to use our voice, which is why we can handle delicate matters with poise.

- The advice given by Google can turn out to be quite brutal. You don't want to get sued, do you? So be careful of what you read and recognize a good source when you see one.

- Stop playing and realize Blockchain is the last train leaving the station. Hesitation creates limitations. Don't miss the train. All aboard!.

- I'm not sure how many get that, Blockchain is in fact the train track. If there are things you'd like to keep and store without going outside of the law, then Blockchain can help those interested.

- Nothing else matters without ladders that lead us to the truth , coupled with relevant evidence and verifiable proof. Blockchain does this too.

- How do you maintain your post and still do what you love to do the most? Easily, by adding potential to your growth.

- Sometimes the best help is just someone giving you tools that you can add to your tool belt.

- Always self-analyze. You want to constantly ask yourself

where are you winning or losing and where do you need to start improving?

- Plus or minus a couple of factors, if you're humble, you'll appear more attractive and less likely to start moving backward.

- Input vs Insight: Lo and behold, I was always told that Input is about influence and insight is about being right - even when it doesn't seem right.

- If you want to intellectually grow as a woman or a man - you're going to need some sort of Growth Plan. A good book is always a good look.

- Women with Power: No matter her potential or whether or not she's influential, very few people will require her to have more credentials. Would you get into a vehicle with a woman who doesn't know where the brakes are ?

- Never negotiate a deal if a person doesn't give you a chance to take a moment to think about the "what if" possibilities well in advance.

- How do you get rid of these "Target Rich Cyber-poor Entities?" By coming up with "Security First" remedies and keeping them in mind. They will likely give you protection over a much longer period of time.

- I find people that are not secure by design are often the ones who get left behind. They can be stuck in a fog, because it becomes that much harder for them to secure a job.

- Do you think a bank could ever desert us? I ask because one of them said, "I don't want a nation of thinkers. I want a nation of workers."

- When your attention span is short like mine, you would do well to take certain people, places, and things with a "grain of salt" sometimes.

- People are usually going to give you money for one of three reasons:

- For what you've read
- For what you've said, or
- For what you've retained in your head

BELIEVE IT OR NOT, THAT'S HOW MOST PEOPLE MAKE their bread.

- Valued information can foster good experiences - whether you read it, heard it, or saw it - if others really want it, believe me, they will hunt you down and pay for it. What I'm saying is this - If your information is legit, people will find you to attain it.

- Whether you say it or you think it, I'm sure you know the saying, "You can lead a horse to the water but you can't make them drink it." It's the lesser known verse that I love:" All you have to do is feed him enough salt and then leave him alone, I promise you, that horse will go and find water on its own."

- Whether it's an OCEAN or a CANOE, there are 5 Big Personality Traits. Of the Big Five, it's always good to know - which one are you?

- A Belief Breakthrough Coach can only be successful using the correct approach.

- Money is something you earn. Favors are something you return. This is both a rule and a fact. You shouldn't ask for one unless you're willing to give the other one back.

- "Growing in love" is ALWAYS better because of what it does. What I can say for certain is "growing in love" gives you an opportunity to learn more about said person.

- Learning is about "doing the math" before deciding to chart a path with a person just because they make you laugh.

- A relationship that is guaranteed to malfunction is a relationship that doesn't have the right fit or function.

- With yourself you may fight because you can't identify what success looks like. Furthermore, you may not know where to begin because you may not know where you should look to win.

- Our taste buds affect how we all learn, grow, laugh, and love. Sometimes thoughts are like sprouts. You're probably wondering what I am talking about. Well when looking at a sprout, depending on what you see, it will determine if you leave it and let it grow to become a tree. Or if you'll kill it before anyone else gets a chance to see?

- In business, you quickly recognize that price is the cost you pay and if the quality is good the customers will stay.

- One of Malcolm X's favorite sayings was "Make it Plain."

It is something that I've adopted in order to reframe certain thoughts that I entertain.

- They say to work smarter and not harder. However when you're working on you– working harder is working smarter.

- A message that I hope I'm sending is that winning is about having data before voicing an opinion.

- Even though at first it might not feel right, quality is probably more important than price. Why?

- Let me just ask you, is it true that based on only

presentation and appearance that you are able to determine whether or not a person has actual experience?

- If you don't do well the first time, then practice harder and maybe the next time you'll go farther.

- There it is. I heard it again. What's that? It's your heart telling your head that you deserve to win. As long as you're a person willing to put the work in.

- How will you respond when you're asked, "Do you always have to excel at what you do?" Are You self aware or do you even have a clue?

- Oh no doubt, I'm happy to give you a chance to banter –

In hopes that together we can come up with the right answer.

- There are always going to be factions that cause distractions. Don't hurt them. Nah, instead convert them by finding out what fuels their passions.

- You can exercise wisdom by breaking the cycle of recidivism. After you mess up, you should try to get up. Anybody who falls down has the right to fight their way back up off the ground.

- Without exaggeration, back in the day the mere thought of being successful was just a figment of my imagination. Not any more though, I proved that I'm not delusional because I was actually able to grow into a PROfessional.

- Question: Are you following a script that you've been given or is your story in the process of being rewritten?

- When you know where you want to go, be careful where you sit. Don't romanticize the destination and completely miss the trip.

- When you have employment and people think that you enjoy it, you might be perceived as successful but flamboyant.

- In an age where being consistent is viewed as being different, even the non-conformist knows the importance of remaining steadfast in their performance.

- We all have a story. No matter how bad it is, let a narrator help you to best narrate your narrative.

- When someone tries to beat you down with words, tell them you don't want to hear it. Whether it's blatant or covert, it's all designed to misdirect, block, and break your spirit.

- Without a seat at the table, how can I possibly and properly defend you? It appears that I'm not at the table because I'm on the menu!

- Certain situations have nothing to do with whether or not they deserve it. It's more about who makes the final decision. The master or the servant? The biggest factor is that the servant is the opposite of an independent contractor. You may say, "What's the difference cousin?

"Well, one controls their own time while the other one doesn't.

• When using my head to make some bread, I know that I can't make bread without having some dough. You've heard this adage that's true even though it sounds funny: It takes money to make money, honey!

- If you've been waiting for your dream to come true, then I advise you to do as the Earth does when it changes its position relative to the Sun - revolve.

- Sometimes when acting in haste, we tend to forget that one hand washes the other and both hands wash the face.

- Why is quality more important than price? It's simple. Just think about quality food and how it impacts your quality of life. Quality food improves your health, while a good quality of life improves your wealth.

- Success: Believe that you're not only going to get it, but that you're also going to attract the people who are able to help you with it.

- People perish from a lack of knowledge. Instead of focusing on what's in our heads, we get distracted and focus on what is in our wallets.

- I consider myself an asset because I answer questions that haven't been asked yet.

- If your preference is excellence then you should read this: When each of us were born, we came with books compiled as a set of instructions. They consist of The Old, New, and Last Testament. The fourth book is written by each of us to cap off such a hefty life investment. Our own Book is the final product that demonstrates our individual excellence.

- Finally, dare I say most importantly, many will sing your praises when you present your unique Book of Words, Definitions and Phrases.

Afterword

Lastly, I want to provide the answer to the question that most people ask me,

How did I do it?

Well I did it with the help of two loving parents who despite public perception, attempted to steer me in the right direction. My parents are nearest & dearest to my heart because there's no one closer. I wake up and try to emulate their courage, while avoiding their errors! You may not have the same high caliber relationship with your parents and that is fine. It really boils down to how and with whom you spend your time.

Identify who is going to take the time to tell you what you need to know in order for you to grow?

Nobody ever pulled me aside as a child and told me,

"Hey listen up Vernon. You think you know what you're doing, but you don't. I'm gonna give you space to make the mistakes that we all make. How well you pull through depends on what you subsequently choose to do. Vernon, when you've grown tired of all the pains, aches, and heartbreaks from not listening, then that's when you'll start

seeking out "different." "Different" includes new information and questions. Each one is an experience, which is why you should always be mindful of your appearance."

Nobody really took the time to tell me this. I am telling you because it is my hope that whatever you're going through, my Book of Words, Definitions & Phrases can help you to see it through . . . one day at a time.

P.E.A.C.E. = Proper Education Always Corrects Errors
Thank YOU for your time.
I am looking forward to reading your book!

BIBLIOGRAPHY

1. Reading At Risk - National Endowment for the Arts (.gov)
https://www.arts.gov/sites/default/files/RaRExec.pdf↑
2. 21 Captivating Reading Statistics and Facts for 2022,
https://comfyliving.net/reading-statistics/
3. THE SEVEN NEIGHBORHOOD STUDY REVISITED
https://static1.squarespace.com/static/58eb0522e6f2e1dfce591dee/t/
596e1246d482e9c1c6b86699/1500385865855/seven-neighborhood+revisited+
rpt.pdf↑
4. Etymology, origin and meaning of mathematics by etymonline; https://www.
etymonline.com/word/mathematics↑
5. Nelson Mandela's Secret to Winning
https://www.inc.com/jim-schleckser/nelson-mandela-s-secret-to-winning.html↑
6. The Beatings Will Continue until Morale Improves
https://quoteinvestigator.com/2020/07/15/morale/↑
7. Rev. DeForest "Buster" Soaries, Jr.'s Story
https://healamericamovement.org/blog/rev-buster-soaries-jr-s-story/↑
8. No Thinkers, I Want Workers
https://medium.com/illumination/no-thinkers-i-want-workers-f28d9de0f7c6↑